THIS BOOK BELONGS TO:

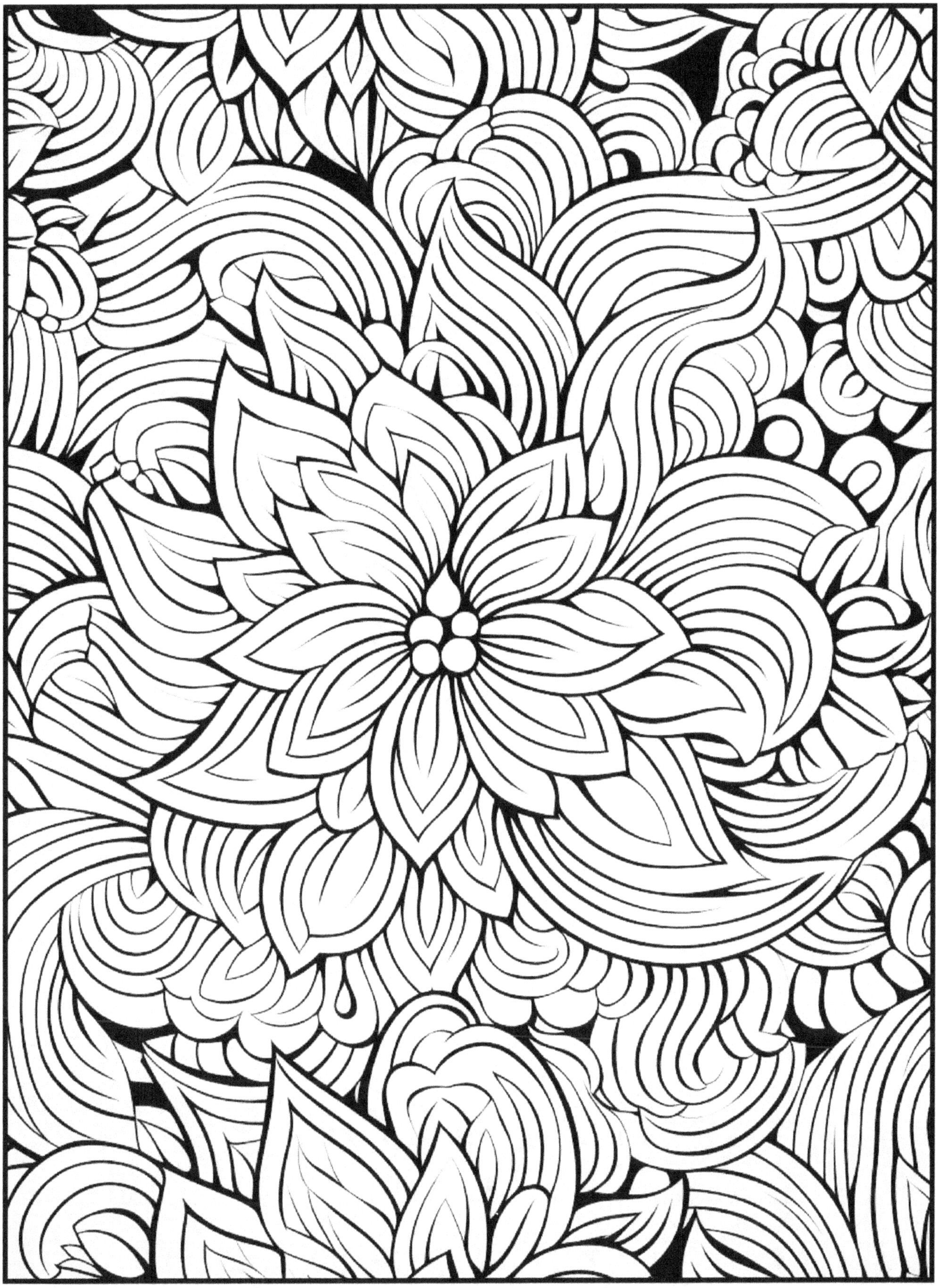

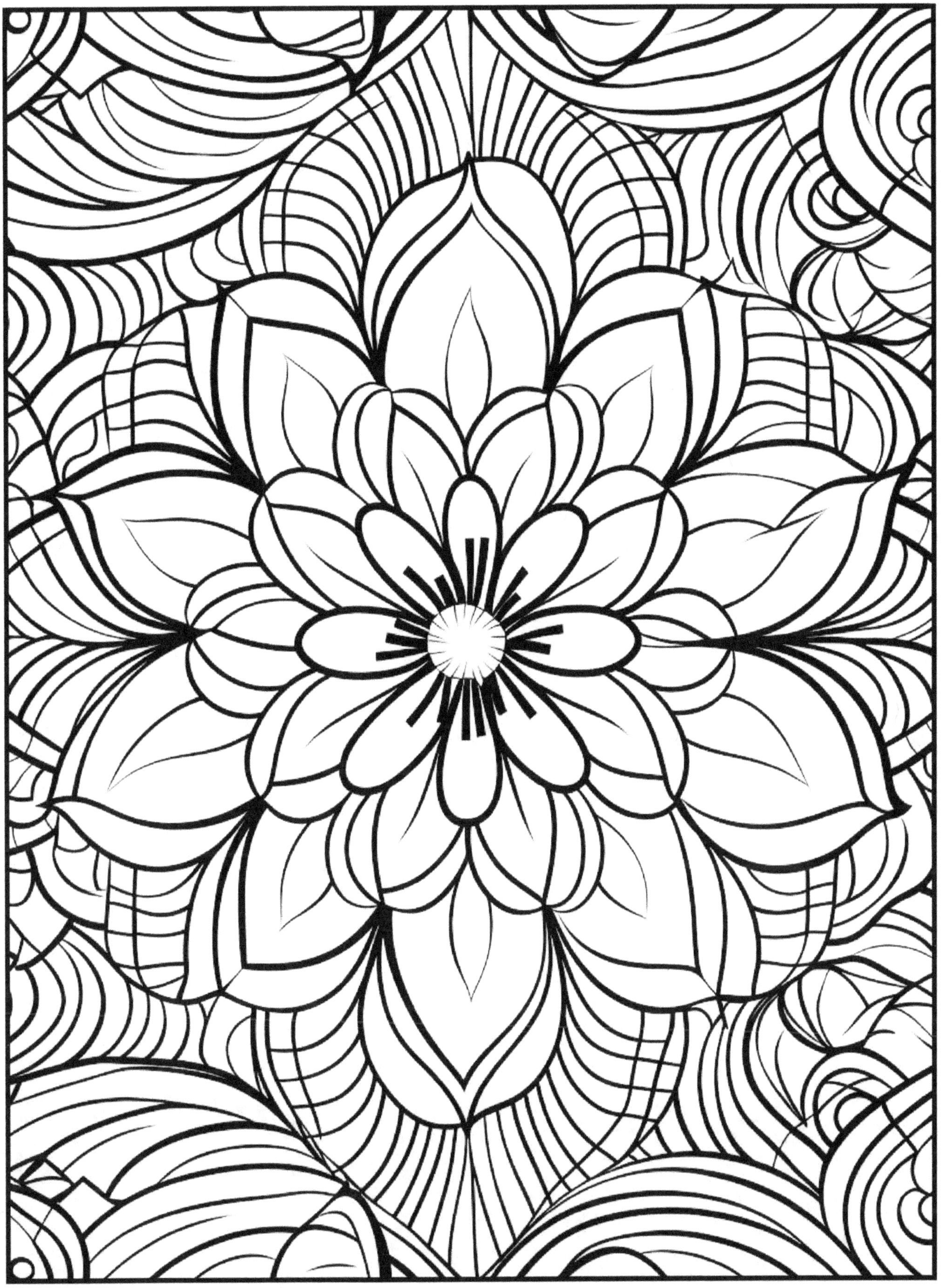

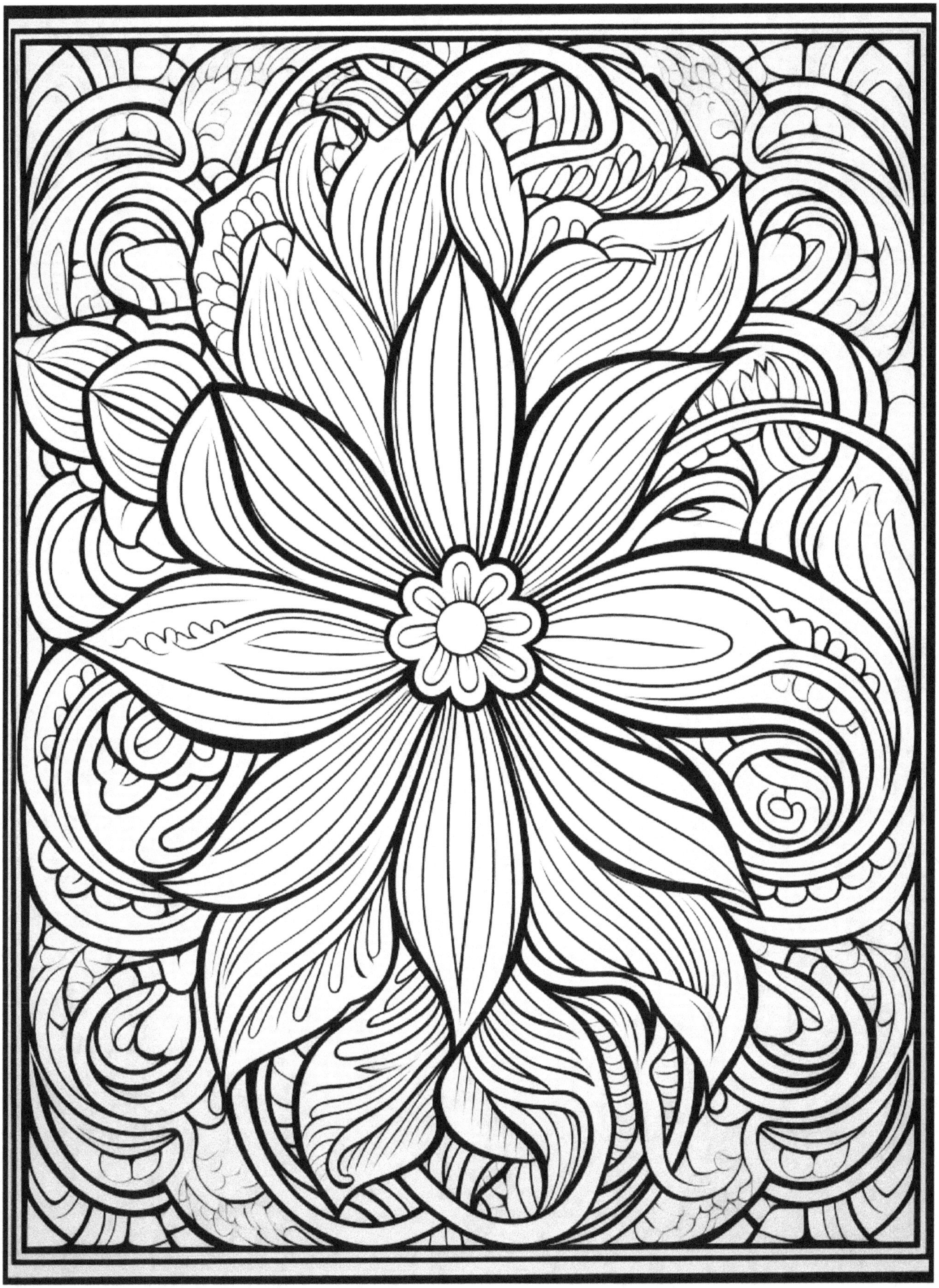

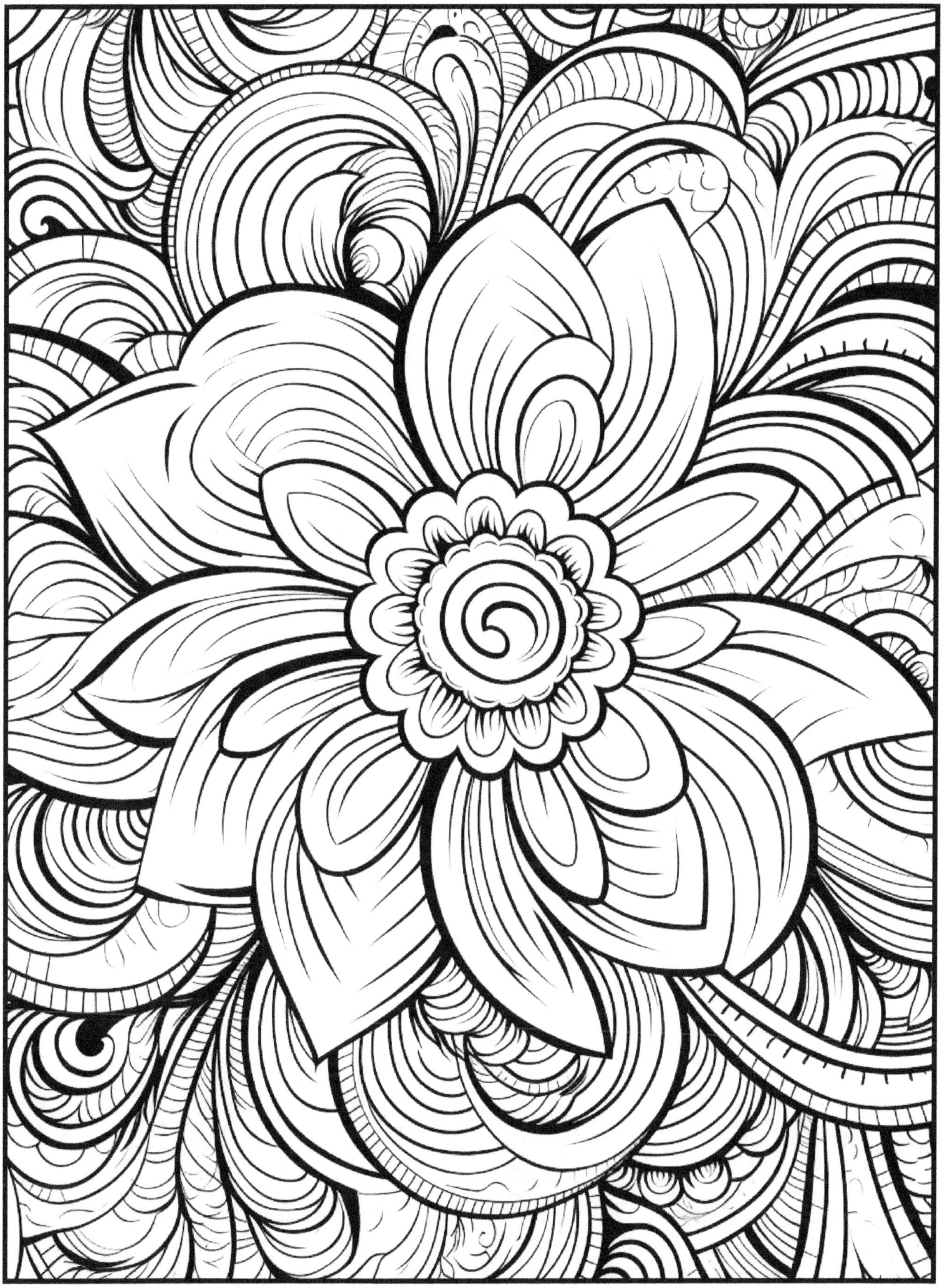

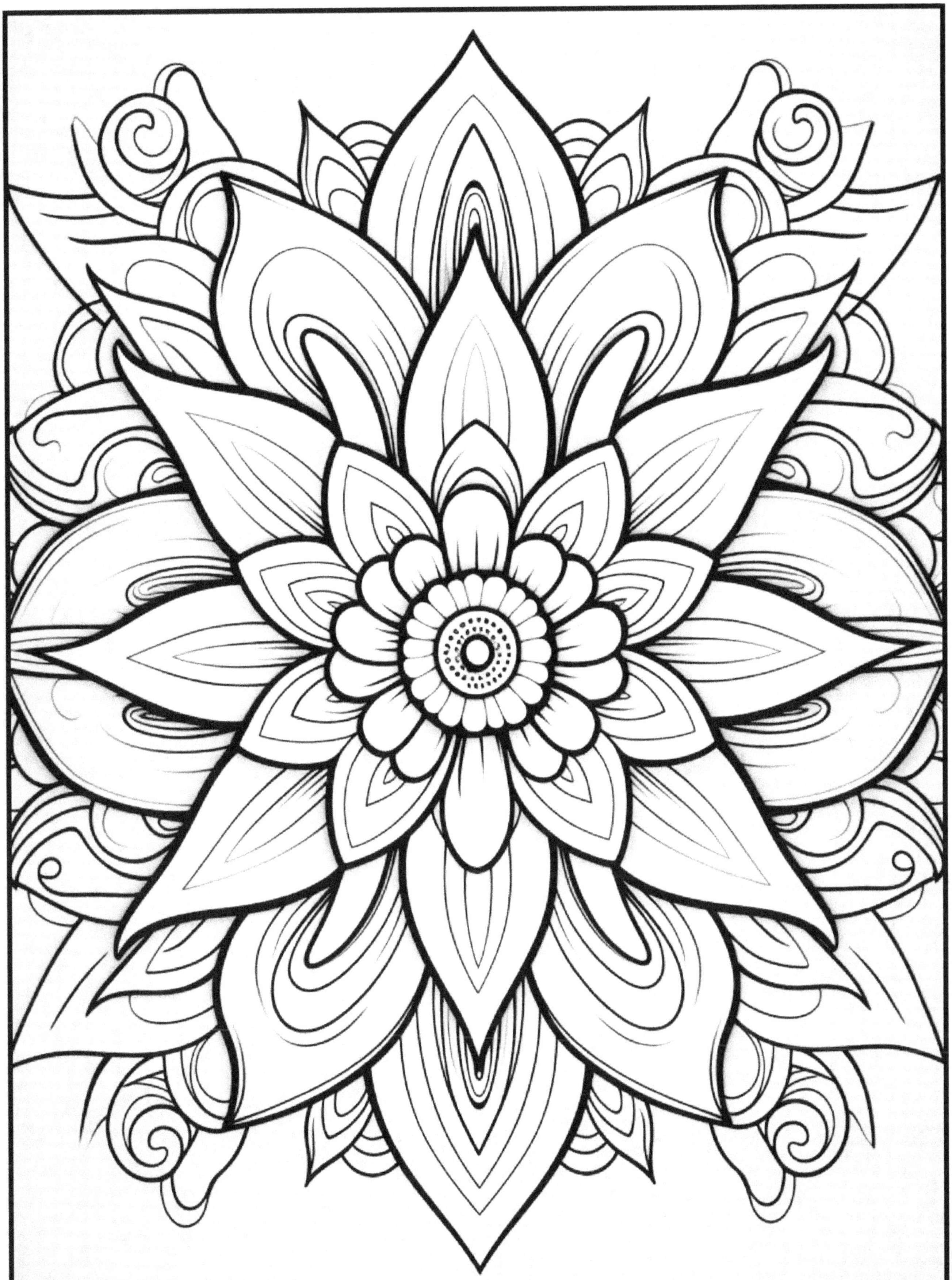

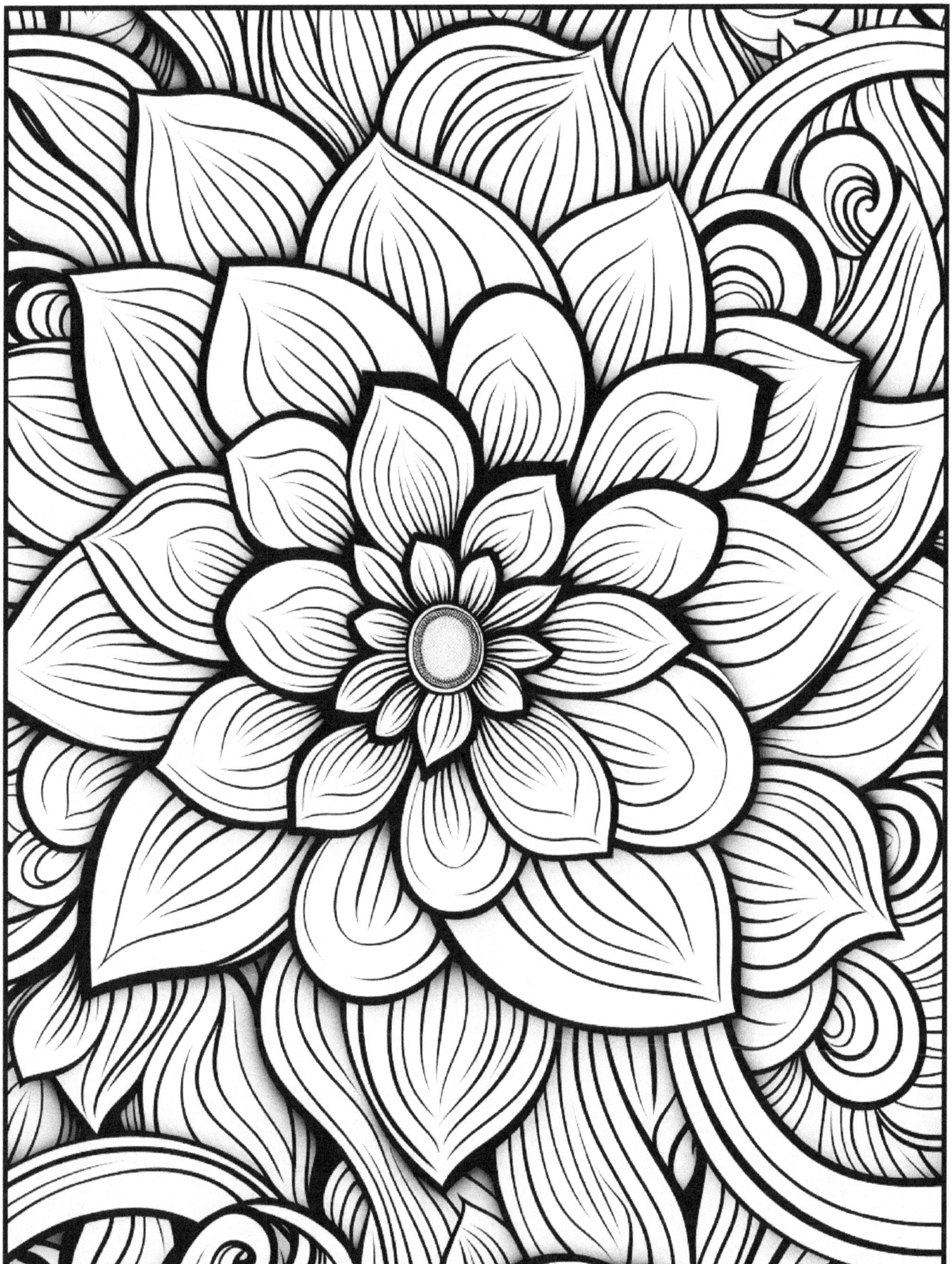

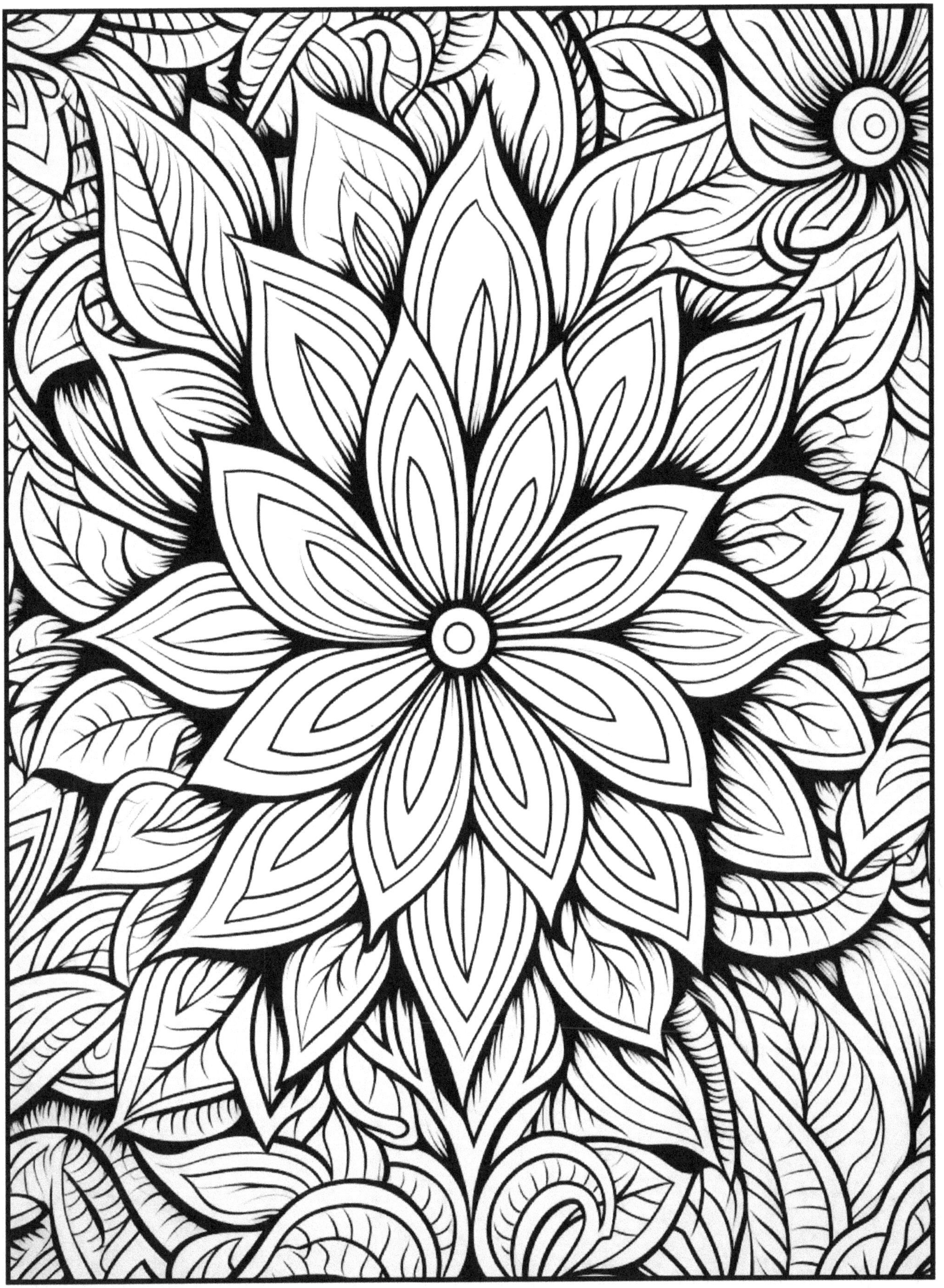

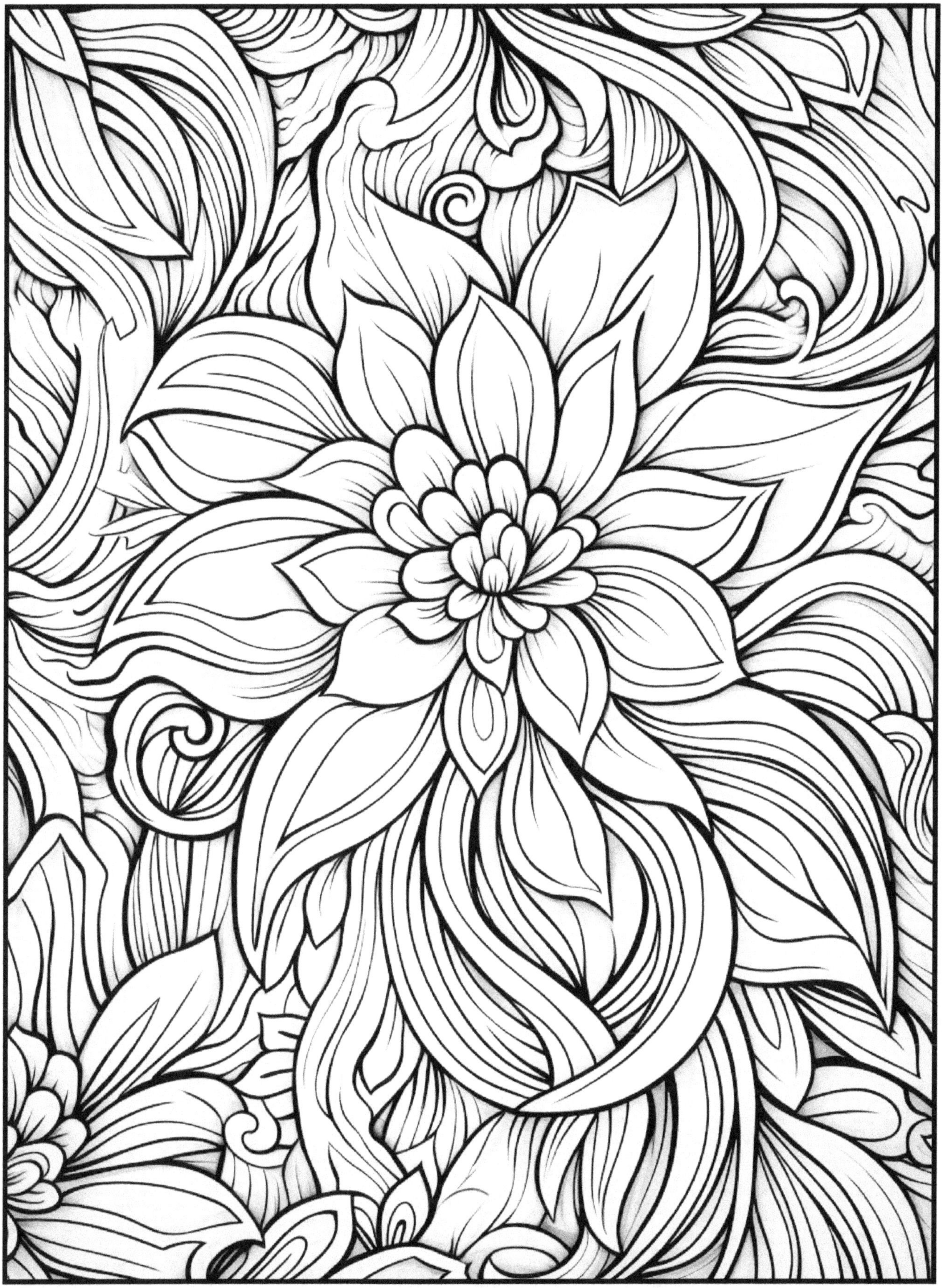

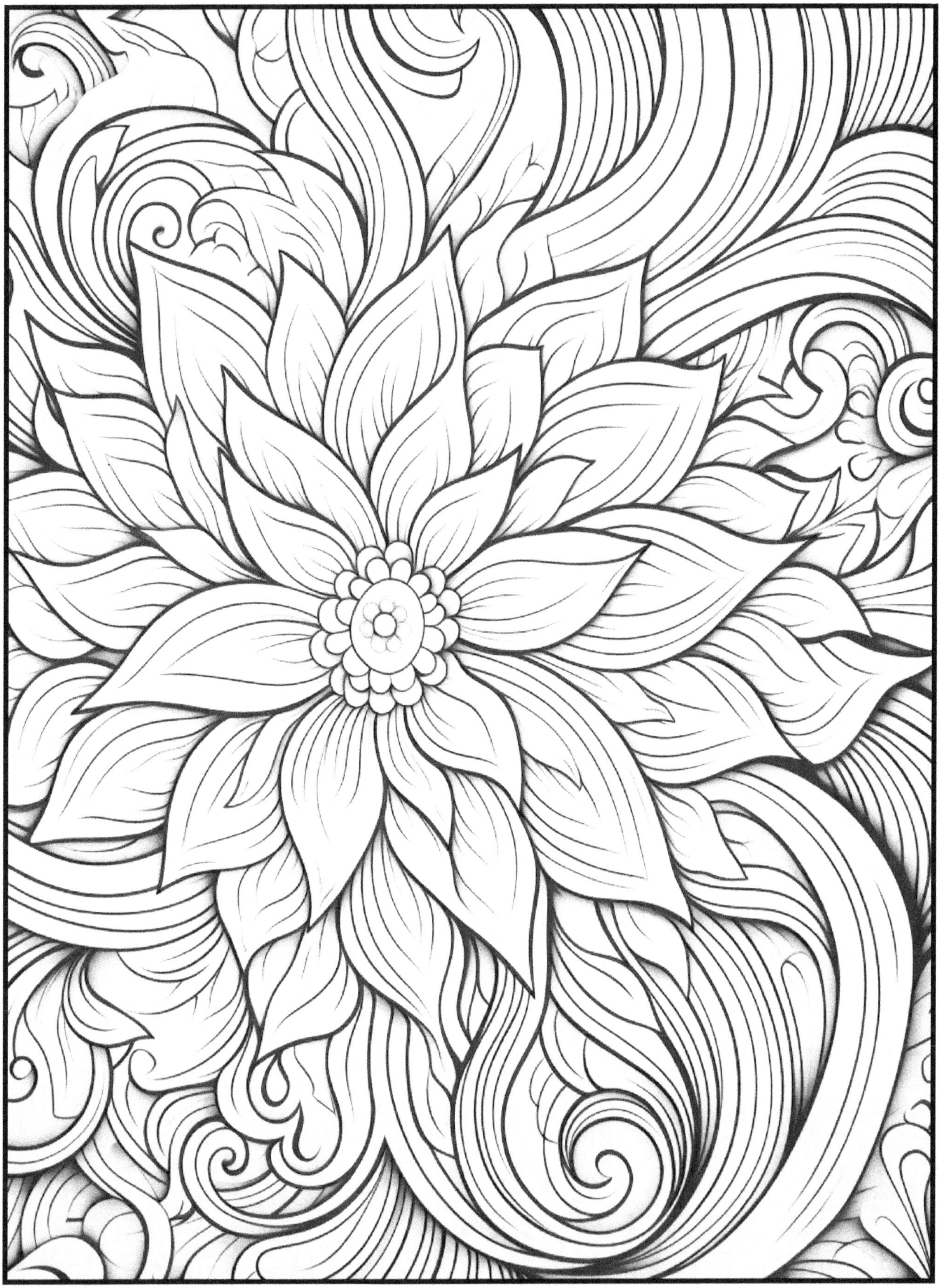

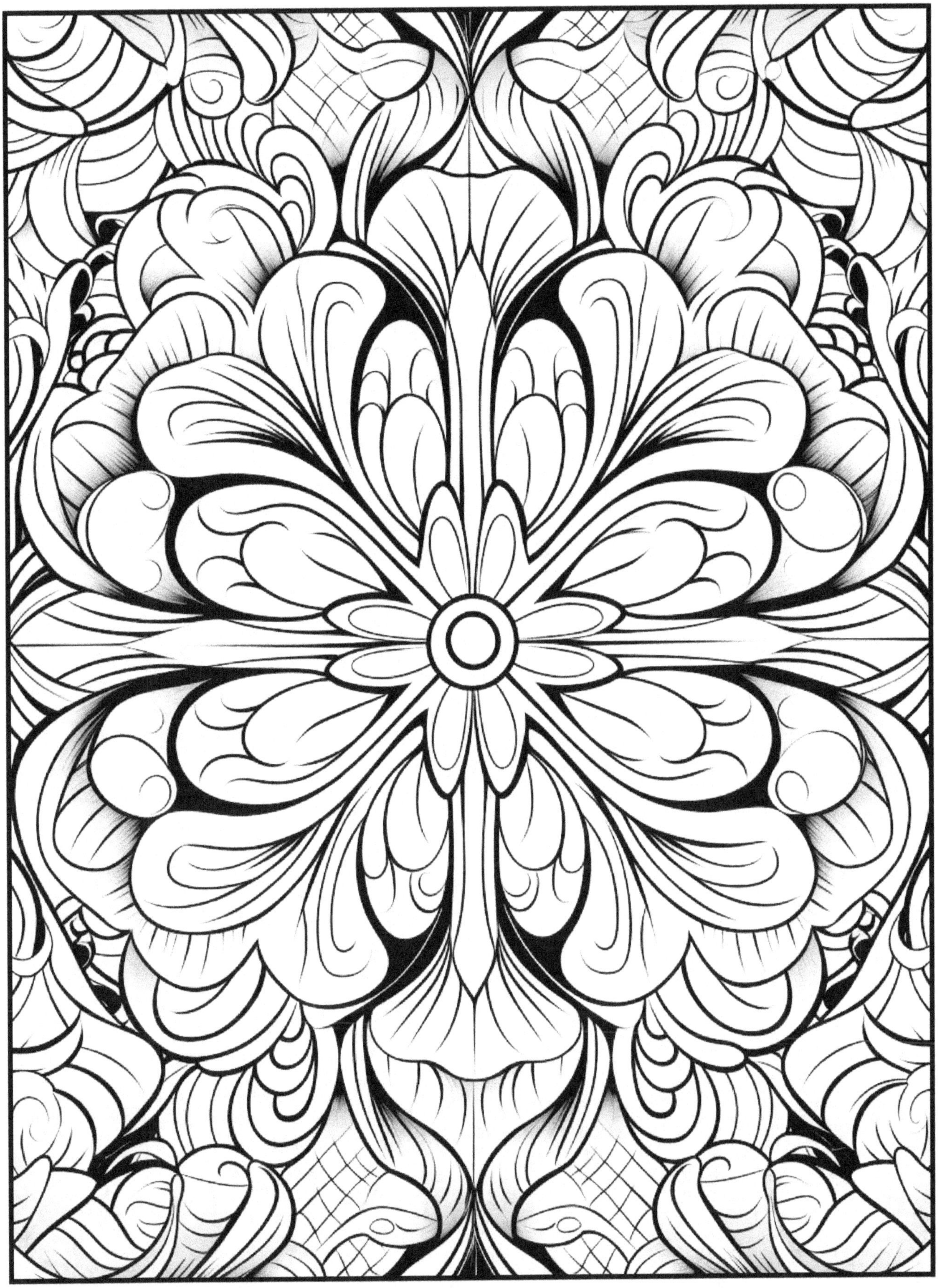

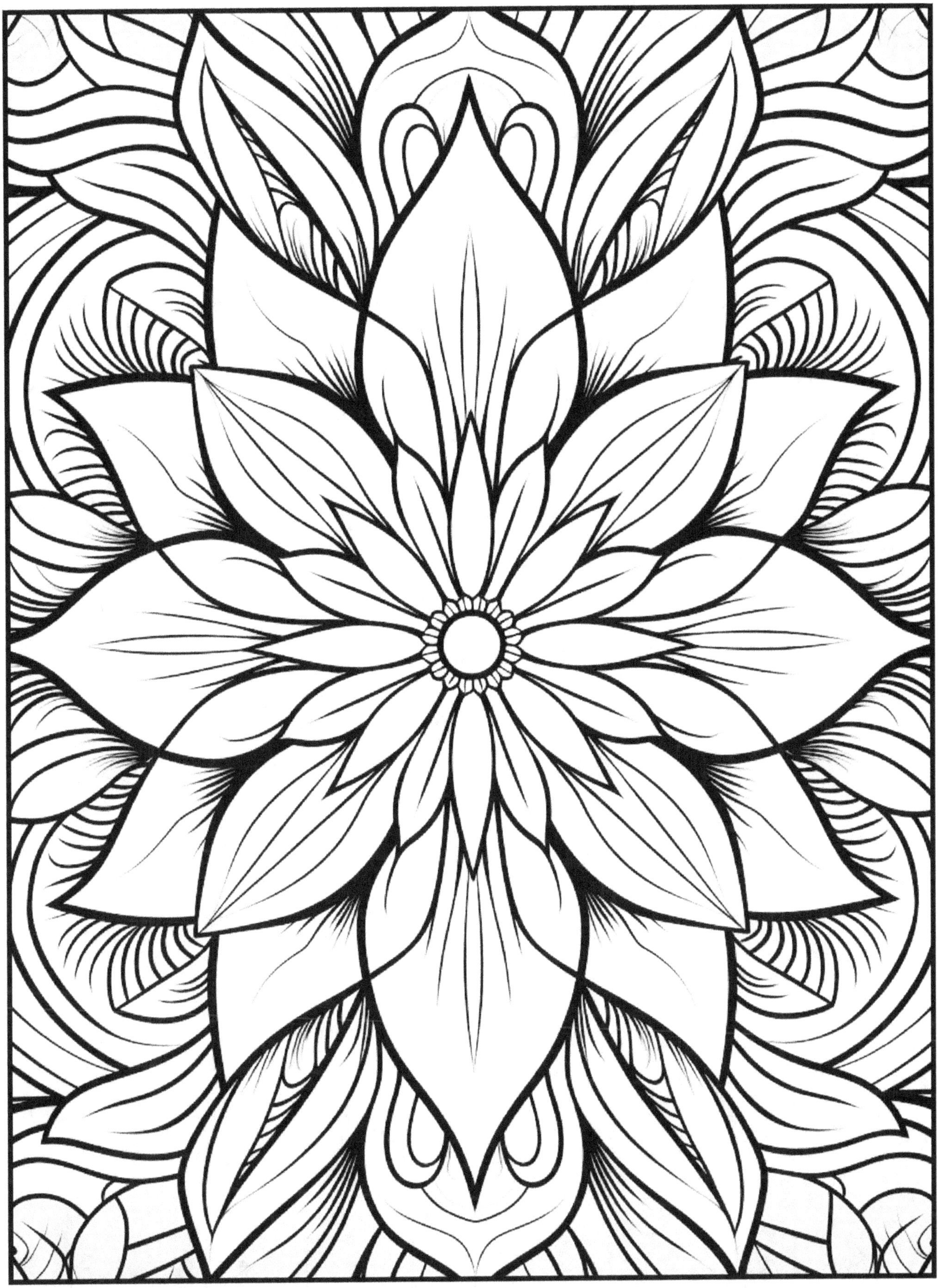

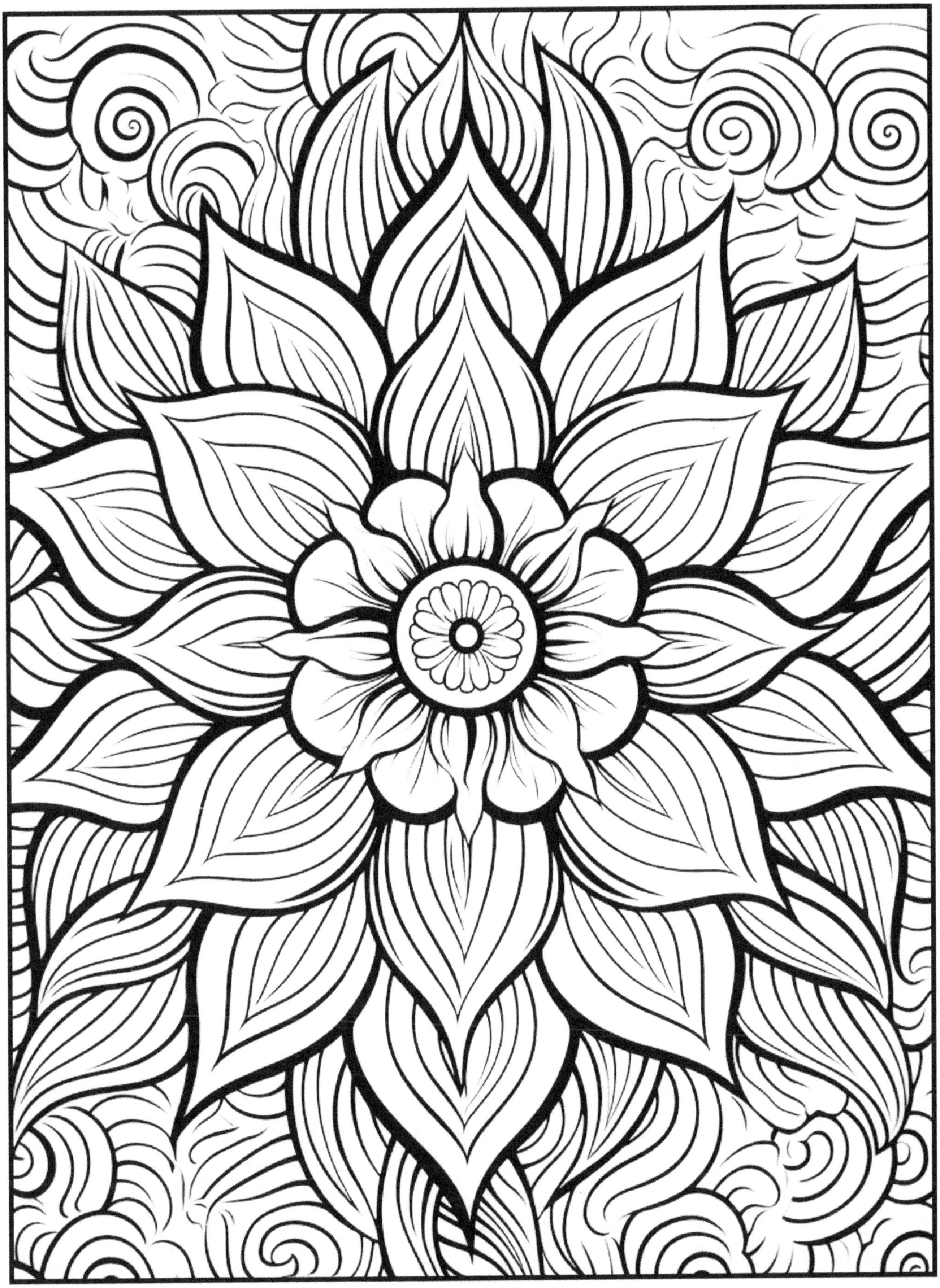

www.ingramcontent.com/pod-product-compliance
Lightning Source LLC
Chambersburg PA
CBHW080957290526
45795CB00009B/2986
9798883635402